TONGUE INK

(Part One)

Written By

LARRY A. YFF

CHAPTERS

1. Marriage   3

2. "Your View Matters" - the book series   21

3. "Your View Matters" - the podcast   32

4. "VIEW" fashion line   40

5. "Kings, Queens and Killers" - the series   50

6. Real Estate Development   55

7. Love and Hate Memoirs (Jonetta Yff)   64

8. Private Matter: You Got That? (Larry Yff)   77

CHAPTER ONE

Marriage

Jonetta Minter and I got married 12/20/2020. Nobody knew about our plans outside of her and me. There was no big wedding ceremony. There was no honeymoon. There was no...you get the point.

Jonetta and I met around 2015. I was new to Muskegon Michigan and had met a lady who I would call my grandma and business partner, Ciggzree S. Morris, through her granddaughter Mia, who I had met a few months earlier. Mrs. Morris attended Mt. Zion COGIC church on Muskegon Ave. and asked me if I wanted to go with her. I went and became a member after the second time going. Jonetta was already a member of Mt. Zion and we met a couple of times at the services and during a church play that we were both in.

We didn't really communicate much until she contacted me to help her put together a bed at her apartment. That was the first time I really got to see her up close and personal and all I really remember is her eyes. Her lips and her eyes. Actually it was her lips her eyes and her nose. She had a certain way of looking at you and telling you exactly what was on her mind with her eyes and her lips, nose and eyebrows all followed with their own gestures that reinforced what her eyes were saying.

For instance, if I said something she thought was corny she didn't have to tell me. Her eyes would slant a little, her eyebrows would scrunch together, her nose would kind of scrunch up too and then her lips would be puckered to the side. I would instantly know, based on those expressive gestures that what I said was either corny, cute, stupid or out of line.

I wanted to kiss her. I remember just wanting to have those eyes invite me closer and then kissing those lips. It never happened. It was all business: I was free to help set up the bed and then leave.

After that I never saw her again or talked to her again until early 2020. She was doing her thing in Detroit and Muskegon and I was living back in Grand Rapids, Michigan. One day I got a message on Facebook from Netta. She asked if I was available to help her move some stuff and was I in town. I rearranged my schedule so I could get there and help. Even though we hadn't talked for years, we somehow instantly vibed. It was like we picked up where we left off even though we hadn't really had anything to *pick up* from.

It was during this time when we would begin to talk on the phone. We didn't necessarily talk about getting together; but we definitely knew something was *there*. I was in a situation at the time and so was she. We both agreed to be straight up and honest from the start if we were even going to be friends. What I liked was when we would talk about business, she remembered me talking about doing real estate development and involving young kids from years ago...and I was still working on that and talking about it. Without me saying certain aspects, she would tell me an idea she had and it would either match what I wanted to do or it somehow would be the perfect addition to what I was planning on doing.

During this initial time, my situation changed and I had my own apartment. She came to see me one time and it was horrible! We hadn't seen each other in years and her first time seeing me I was smoking crack. Yup. Something about her wanting to come to town and see me gave me anxiety and I called my dude and started getting high. I told her just come a different day. She said she was already on the way and that shot my anxiety even higher!

All I remember is she calling me and texting me saying she was outside and wanted to come in. I would text her back and say something like, "Just wait there. I went to the store and will be back in a minute." I knew she didn't believe me, but I was looking for excuses to continue getting high and continue to avoid her seeing me like this. It didn't work.

After her blowing her horn in the front of my house several times, then blowing it in the back of the house, then ringing the front doorbell and knocking on the back door...I finally opened the door. Well, I actually saw her out front and texted she to let her know the back door was open. Hearing her come in and walk into my room and seeing me high crushed my soul. It hurt. I was embarrassed and felt like shit. I felt stupid. I felt like she would never want to see me again in life...and I just wanted to block it all out and finish smoking.

She was, as to be expected, disappointed; but we still chatted a little bit. I don't remember how long. She even asked me if I was hungry and ordered some chicken for us. I played it off like I was hungry; but I really just wanted her to leave me alone. I wanted to finish my drugs and my pity party. She sat in my living room and ate a couple of pieces of chicken; while I sat on my bed looking like a scolded little boy. After she finished her meal alone, I walked her out, she left and I finished getting high.

That's the thing about addiction. People like to tell you to just stop. When I'm in the middle of it, I was never able to just stop. I had to go until I either ran out of money or whoever's house I was at had to tell me I had to leave. Since I was high, I knew what I looked like and what I was doing was wrong and at the same time, nothing matters while there's drugs to be smoked. It didn't matter if I hurt her feelings or if I would never see her again in life. I would deal with that when it was time to come off my high and deal with reality. That's the reality of the addiction I had.

Fast forward to September of 2020. My friend Mia called and asked me to come to Muskegon and do some work renovating houses. I was excited. She picked me up from Grand Rapids and took me to Muskegon. It was another fucking disaster in my life!

I stayed in an apartment that her home-repair team had recently fixed up. She had plenty of work and we were both excited to get started. The first week or so was fine. After that, I began to get that itch and started smoking crack again. She knew what I was doing, but was stuck between being my friend and telling me to stop and being my friend and letting me be a grown-ass man.

Eventually, we had to part ways because I was getting high waaaaay too much. There were times where I would be up all night getting high and when she would come to pick me up, I would give her some lame excuse about how I was still tired from yesterday. She gave me multiple chances to work and it was no use. I had fallen into another bad routine and was quickly dropped from the team.

During this time I still had a sense that God was with me. I had prayed years ago and asked God to take this addiction away from me and He said, "No. If I just take it away from you, I won't be able to use your testimony to help millions of others see how following My laws can lead to a better way of living and I won't be able to show the world how My laws can help them overcome something as devastating as crack addiction." With that in mind, I slowed down. I assessed my situation and looked for the lesson like I always did; eventually I found it.

That trip to Muskegon was the first time in my life I had ever directly worked with the pure motive being to smoke crack. I had worked before and spent some of my check getting high, but it wasn't the first or only thing on my mind. *This* time around, I literally worked all day, got high all night and went to work off 2 hours of "sleep" and at the end of that day, take my day's pay and go get high all over again. You may think there was no lesson and that I was just getting high but no...there was a lesson: I now understood how degrading and how de-humanizing and un-manly it felt to live on your own and smoke crack/do drugs every day. I knew firsthand how insignificant and depressed it gets. I knew firsthand what it takes to try and tell yourself that you're still a man even though you 1) don't feel like one, 2) you know you are a fuckup, 3) everybody around you views you as a fuckup and 4) as long as you are able to get the job done...nobody really gives a fuck.

    I used to sell a lot of drugs. I clearly remember the power I felt when I got a hold of some grown ass man with an addiction and I could tell him to cut my grass for a $20 rock or wash me and my friend's cars for a $20 rock. It felt good to have somebody "needing" me. It felt good controlling somebody else. Females with drug addictions were always ready to give up the ass cheap for some drugs. People all of a sudden thought I was a good guy and all my jokes were funny. I could talk to a "crackhead" however I wanted and he wouldn't say shit; because if he did, I would cut him off and not front him any more dope. I had a sense of power when somebody would call me for some drugs and I would make them wait and put them on my schedule. There is a power you get from being a drug-dealer and it's the same power a lot of politicians and rich people have: 1) somebody needs me, 2) I'm better than somebody else and 3) I have power over someone else's lifestyle. After this experience, when I do any type of business, especially in the home repair arena where addiction is fed because it's often wages paid in cash and under the table, I will pay a worker what he or she is worth regardless of their situation. I will not take advantage of someone's addictive lifestyle. Lesson learned.

While I was going through the ups and downs of getting high, Netta still kept in contact with me. In fact, she kept in contact with me as much as possible on a daily basis. There were times she would have a meal ready for me and we would have plans for the night...I would cancel by default because I had gotten high that night. I'm highlighting a lot of addiction episodes not to make excuses or whatever; instead it's to show you how Netta and my relationship started off and stayed strong at a time when the average woman would have left.

I was a mess. Since I was no longer working for my friend, I decided it was only right to move out the apartment she had for me. Where I was going to go was a crap shoot. It was the same day I planned on moving that Netta called me and told me to pack my things. She said, "Get everything you want because you are going to stay with me." I was living in the moment and felt relief. She and I hadn't officially become an item yet; but this move catapulted us in the right direction.

We had many nights of talking and sharing personal trials in life that brought us close. Finding out that both of her parents had been addicted to and died from drug-related health issues was major. Those years had actually equipped her with the ability to see the humanity in me still. There were a couple of times where I was living with her and had gone missing-in-action. When I would explain to her how I felt there was something spiritual attached to my addiction, the spiritual side of her was able to accept it. We became inseparable. She was the first person who actually believed me when I told her the story about asking God to take away my addictions and His response.

I was able to see and know things about her not many people knew or had seen. We had our private life together with secrets that we were willing to share with one another.

She realized she had areas in her life she wanted to work on and we both accepted each other for it. Not in an enabling type way. It was in a way that made us closer and got both of us closer to God. Once again, it was our common spiritual view that when the Bible tells us to openly confess our sins to one another so we can help each other, we took that leap of faith and did it and it worked.

We started living together in September and talks of marriage started around November. Neither one of us was interested in the big wedding and spending thousands of dollars for one day of celebrating. We were both more interested in doing the act of marriage vows in front of God. This was during the Covid19 scare and churches, schools, restaurants, everybody was shut down. We went to the City Clerk's office and got a list of pastors who were willing to do a wedding ceremony in real life as opposed to a Zoom or Skype wedding. We called her and told her we wanted to get married and that we wanted to do it on December 30 in a gesture of acknowledging my parents who had gotten married on that date about 60 years ago and were still married.

Oh wait. The proposal. One day she asked me if I was serious about marrying her and I said "yes." She stared at me with that intense look and then walked off into the kitchen or somewhere in the house. I remember thinking to myself that I didn't want to wait and if you have a good thing you shouldn't wait. "Hey baby. Come here for a second." She came in the room and I said, "Will you marry me?" She said, "So I'm assuming this is your proposal??" I said, "Yup" and she said "yes". That was how the proposal went.

Ok, now we are back to setting our date. We have the church secured and are looking to do it at the end of December, 2020. I'm not sure who initiated the conversation, but somehow we got to talking about marriage and the topic of "why wait" came up. We both agreed to just do it now and we called the pastor back and asked if we could do it that weekend I believe. She said we should come to the service that Sunday and she could do it afterwards. We told her we would see her Sunday.

I called my parents and told them I was getting married and wanted them to come and be the two witnesses. They came and witnessed the wedding, signed their names and gave us a wedding gift of a bag with treats including one of my favorites, Dutch Honey bread! My best man was a guy I met at Guiding Light Rehab in Grand Rapids, Michigan named Jeremy Anderson. I always forget his name because his nickname was "Coach". We were roommates for a little while and got along pretty good. Actually, I have to backtrack and tell you about him.

They say you never know someone until you live with him or her. He and I were cool...until we lived together. It took us a while to settle in and become actual friends. I remember the first night I was laying on my bed listening to some music in my headphones trying to fall asleep. I'm awoken when he is pulling off my headphones. I look at him and say, "What tha fuck are you doing?" and he calmly said, "I'm taking your headphones off your head because I asked you to turn it down and you didn't." I was like, this dude got some balls!!

I'm in rehab and I don't want to get kicked out for fighting; especially something as small as that. Since I was up now and couldn't sleep, I grabbed some chips and laid back down with my headphones turned down...slightly. Next thing I knew, he had come over to my bed and was tapping me on my chest!! "Yo, Coach. Leave me tha fuck alone dude. I'm serious!!" I tell him. He was un-phased and said, "Why do you have to chew so loud! Look at you! You have chips and crumbs all over your chest! You eat like a pig! How about you eat something soft at night or chew with your mouth closed!" And then he went back to his bed as if everything he did was normal. That was my first night actually getting to know him. We became closer after that and only had one other incident. After I got kicked out of Guiding Light we still kept in contact. Four months later, my friend and best-man Coach would be dead from an overdose.

    At the time of this writing, Netta and I have been married for exactly seven months. I just realized it is July 20, 2021! I highly recommend marriage…and not because she just happened to walk by and is looking over my shoulder. There are things that happen in marriage that don't happen anywhere else. We actually almost divorced about 4 times; mostly within the first 2 months or so. I would never go back to dating again if I had to. Intentionally making a commitment to each other in front of God gave us a fear and respect that trumps anything we have going on in our relationship. I won't go into a ton of details, but the mutual respect we have for each other personally and spiritually has spilled over into our business life together and has made it an amazing journey.

This book is about how our marriage was and is the foundation of our business life.

CHAPTER TWO

"Your View Matters" - the book series

Around 2017 I had to take a hard look at my life. It was a shit-show! I sat down and made several journals about my life in attempts to figure out how it had gotten so messed up. I grew up in a two-parent household to parents who had been married for 50-plus years without incident of cheating, had a private-school education (Oakdale Christian and then Grand Rapids Christian High), went to a Catholic college (Aquinas College) and now was addicted to drugs, pornos and strippers, had been to jail and prison numerous times, didn't have a career and was still fucking up while I was writing the journals trying to figure out how my life got so fucked up.

I was watching television and something came on about "why you should write a book" and the Holy Spirit gave me that nudge. It's the same nudge that some people say is their 6th sense or their dead granny talking to them. Anyways, the Holy Spirit gave me that nudge and I listened. I began to write a book and that book turned into an 11-book series. The point of this chapter is to show you in more detail how things work out when you just do it.

Once I learned the Holy Spirit knows the future, I began to listen and act instantly. Here's the stages of how the book series got started so you can see the "coincidences":

1. The autobiography was called "Your View Matters".
2. I wrote the second book called "Kings, Queens and Killers" and noticed I can list my book as a series.
3. The autobiography gets changed to "White, Confused, Black and Christian – the Autobiography of Larry A. Yff".
4. I name the series "Your View Matters".

5. The Holy Spirit guides me to write an explicit version of my book because it will appeal to a whole different crowd and the "White, Confused, Black and Christian – the Autobiography of Larry A. Yff" (Explicit Version) is born.

6. I get fed up with the gentrification I see around Grand Rapids, Michigan and the Holy Spirit leads me to write a book for a better, faith-based investment process called "Anthroveration". "Anthroveration" is a term I coined. It basically instructs investors how to incorporate the study of anthropology (anthro), then verify the current residents plight (ver) and then take positive action (adding "tion" to a word makes it an action term).

7. The Holy Spirit nudges me one day while I'm reading internet posts about life coaches and seeing all the talk about personal development stuff. I write "Your View Matters: Personal

Development Plan" by taking the autobiography and "Kings, Queens and Killers" and personalizing a set of questions to answer after reading each book and put it all "under one roof" in the Personal Development Plan. At this point I am getting very excited!

8. The Holy Spirit says to me, "How about an explicit version of the Personal Development Plan for the other audience?" and now "Your View Matters: Personal Development Plan" (Explicit Version) is birthed.

9. Now I am simply listening to my Holy Spirit-guided inner voice and do whatever He says and just sit back in amazement!

10. The Holy Spirit says, "Since 'Anthroveration' is a business book, why not use the same process for that as you did for 'Kings, Queens and Killers'?"

That question birthed "Your View Matters:

Business Development Plan" in the base and the explicit versions.

11. I want to make a note that at this time, I have only sold about 10 copies of all these books total. When people hear I wrote some books, they ask how many have I sold. With a confidence from God that there is a plan for all this writing, I would boldly say "10". At which point people would always tell me how to market it and what I should be doing and I always tell them, "Thanks but no thanks. It will happen on God's time and not mine." My response often made people roll their eyes and talk shit about how I don't know what I'm doing etc.

12. While I'm scrolling through LinkedIn, I notice a lot of people are suddenly experts on cultural diversity and are posting about it, getting degrees in it and holding seminars. The Holy Spirit gave me

that nudge and said, "Most of these people are riding the wave and have no idea what they are talking about. I think you would be good at teaching and writing on cultural diversity. What do you think?" This led me to writing "White Power. Black Pride: Couples Therapy". It's a book that gives the reader a basic, yet in depth, understanding of the root cause for the need to focus on cultural diversity in the World. Couples Therapy refers to the need for black and white people to sit down together and work things out; similar to a husband and wife going to couples therapy.

13. I'm thinking that this is cool to have a cultural diversity plan BUT that was my plan...not God's. The Holy Spirit led me to coin a term called "value retention plan". Cultural diversity is based on how you value people; especially in the workplace.

Once you are able to create a solid plan on how you value people, places and things you will be able to go in any setting and *retain* that set of values no matter where you go; thus the "Your View Matters: Value Retention Plan" was born with the similar process of taking the autobiography and "White Power. Black Pride" to make a base version and an explicit version of the Plan.

14. At this point I am excited, calm with a splash of "when is this gonna happen God". I never thought about writing books and at this stage I have written an entire series with basically zero in sales. I remember now applying the principle I love to call on (Jesus said "You don't have what you want because first off, you haven't been bold enough to ask and second off it doesn't give God glory. Whatever you ask of me that you want to do that

will give God glory...I personally guarantee it will get done.") and asked Jesus to make the books in this series the most widely sold books in the World. I also asked that each Plan book be the best-seller in its respective class in the World. Even though I hadn't sold more than 20 at this time, I felt that calm before the storm knowing what I requested would come to life. This was because the goal was not to make millions, the goal was to help people understand God and the beauty and power of following His laws...the money would come as a result of that and would also be used to give God glory (more details on that later).

15. All of those books were self-published by 2019 I believe. Around February of 2020 the Holy Spirit led me to write "Monkey's Blood: Understanding Your Destiny". I got the nudge to write this book

after scanning YouTube and seeing all the dumb ass shows where "experts" try their hardest to say there is no way God is real, that Jonah's whale was really a submarine, that humans come from monkeys or that somehow science proved you can have a big ass explosion and the Earth somehow is the only planet that came through with all the elements life needs to survive (an explosion blows shit up with no kind of order by the way). I had a need to let people know that if you fall for the story that humans and monkeys share the same bloodline, that you are completely missing out on your beauty and purpose in life as a custom-designed human being.

16. Then in early July of 2021, I was nudged again to write. "The Beginner's Guide to Sinning" came as a result of talking to a new friend about homosexual activity. Him and I sharing our views

on what we thought sin and God was without getting mad or offended.

17. That brings us to date, July 20, 2021. I was moved to write this book even though I have no title yet for it. The nudge came when I was thinking about marriage and how Netta and I have made a lot of business and personal moves the average person would have walked away from; especially when the business moves haven't produced financially yet.

Those 17-points are all I will write about regarding the books, but it's not the end of their purpose. I had learned that when God is sponsoring your activities, He will help you use a creative side like He has. I was enjoying making something special and unique. We all like to do that when it comes to the way we do our hair or our job. Creatively expressing ourselves through love, our clothing and other things brings us joy in life. These books had become my joy whether I made a sale or not. The book series becomes the cornerstone of the podcast, the fashion line and the proposed television series. How the books and those things seamlessly mesh will be covered in the next chapters.

CHAPTER THREE

"Your View Matters" - the podcast

I got kicked out of Guiding Light Rehab in December of 2019. I was devastated. I had been to one other rehab and was disappointed. This rehab was excellent. They were serious about recovery and I loved their process. They believed that recovery from addiction involved spiritual, mental and physical reconstruction of an individual. We would go to the gym 3-4 times a week to stay in shape physically. We met with a spiritual advisor and a life coach weekly as well.

Once you graduate the base recovery program, the new director had it set up where you move into a newly-furnished transition transitional apartment. The new director came from the business world and had a system where the recovery program bought and refurbished multi-family units for the graduating recovery clients. Prior to getting into one of these apartments, the client gets help finding employment. He saves up a set amount of money and then moves into the apartment where all the units are filled with other graduates at various stages of addiction recovery.

I was one week away from graduating the base recovery program, about to enter the employment stage when my actions resulted in expulsion. I moved back in with a good friend of mine and had no idea what was going to happen next in my life. In my limited view, I literally felt like my life was over.

I got on the internet in search of something…anything. I wasn't a big fan of podcast, but one caught my attention and I listened to it. The Holy Spirit gave me that nudge again and said, "Why don't you do a podcast? People are making them every day and talk about anything. You can share your story."

So I asked an associate who had a podcast how to get started. She gave me the basics and I set it up.

Remember, I hated podcasts. I thought it was an overpopulated field with people claiming to be experts on everything and nothing under the sun. It was a cluster-fuck of idiots as far as I was concerned. At this time I had learned to just do what the Holy Spirit tells me and it will somehow be linked to something either now or in the near future. What to name the podcast? Since it would be based on the book, I called it, "White, Confused, Black and Christian – the Podcast". I was super excited that I had another avenue to express myself. Even though it was based on the book series, I didn't know how it would all tie in…yet. What I did know from doing the books is that if you are doing something that will give God glory, the Holy Spirit will guide you to do things that will make your project stand out amongst the crowd. I was excited to see how this podcast thing would unfold.

Here I am with a podcast app on my phone in January of 2020. I am literally rambling and talking about whatever comes to mind. Here's how the whole podcast episode worked:

1. The first month I did 10 episodes and was ecstatic! I felt like this platform had a purpose: helping people with addictions and other issues be bold and open about them and defeat the problems using my life example as the process template. I enjoyed being honest about smoking crack and watching porn till my eyeballs fell out their sockets. There was no shame and helping others be bold and honest and understand their purpose in life was to me, an honorable topic for a podcast.
2. I heard a podcast with music in the background. The Holy Spirit gave me that nudge and said, "That music sounds good. Why don't you have

any?" I researched it, figured out how to do it and not only edited the first episodes, I rattled off another 15 or so epi's in the next month with a musical intro and outro.

3. The excitement is real! By the end of April I had around 40 epi's. I browsed other episodes again and saw some had a picture with each episode. The Holy Spirit said, "Why doesn't yours have any pics?" Once again I researched it and figured out how to do it. I had to go all the way back to Episode 1 and redo all 40 episodes I had to date and put a picture on them and loved the new look!

4. I had gotten up to around 90 epi's around August of 2020. I was in Heaven! I was amazed that I made a podcast from scratch and had 100 epi's in a year! I was watching a show on YouTube about the lifestyles of billionaires.

During the episode, the host recommended a book. The book was "The Richest Man in Babylon". Since I liked the podcast content, I took her advice and bought the book. The Holy Spirit nudged me. "You bought that book because the podcast had good content and the recommended book adds additional and helpful information huh? If you think your podcast has good content, why don't you add a clip about your book? You have multiple books that can help people. Why don't you let the listener know about your helpful books?" I now had to go back through all 90 or so books and add an intro clip that told the listener what book had helpful information in addition to the advice from the epi.

At the end of that year, 2020, I had a podcast that I enjoyed making with approximately 200 episodes. I had fun making it. I had to go through several changes, but it was easy and fun. It wasn't work because I knew from the book writing experience that it would achieve its goal: helping people live a better life with the following of the Bible. It was therapeutic and offered honest advice from brutally honest examples in my life.

The autobiography goes into lots of details regarding me being black and adopted into a white family and the feelings I went through. I honestly spoke on my shortcomings as a dad, son and employee. I gave true examples of the chaos from drug addiction and violence that were the results of going against God's basic laws in the Bible. I was able to do it and not work super hard. Following the Holy Spirit made it easy and fun. Taking the books and podcast experiences into another arena added a whole new level of fun and enjoyment in life I hadn't dreamed of or thought possible: the private-label fashion line.

CHAPTER FOUR

"VIEW" fashion line

Growing up, fashion wasn't a big deal for me. My favorite tee shirt was light green and had the dark green sleeve and neck trim with a front design that read, "Keep on truckin'". My big sister Tammie had a boyfriend who gave me an old pair of his Chuck Taylor's and I loved them! They were old and gold-colored and a couple sizes too big. I didn't care. They were cool and fashionable enough for me.

When the Holy Spirit began to give me ideas about fashion I was mixed. I know fashion can be a crazy arena. Take a plaid shirt and sell it for $20. Add the name "Tommy" on it, and the exact same shirt sells for $110. In fact, the entire fashion industry disgusted me. People sell clothes in America and Europe for $400; while they are paying workers in some less established areas of the world $10 a day or some other ungodly cheap amount. At the same time, I didn't understand how the European fashion scene was able to decide what the gold-standard for fashion in the whole world was. You mention it's a design from Paris or France and the price is sky-high...nobody in the high-end circles of fashion give credit to African American designers or Africa or any "brown" country for that matter. The whole vibe disgusted me.

Around January of 2020, the Holy Spirit began to give me "fashion nudges". My disgust for the either bland European designs or the gaudy designs of the high-class designers made my ass itch every time I saw a commercial toting them as being the top of the fashion world. I wanted to change it.

Since I was doing the books and podcast for God's glory, it was natural when I was led to design a tee shirt with a Bible verse on it. It sounded simple and preachy at first; but the Holy Spirit led me to make it fashionable in its own right. One of my first designs said "Plant-Based Nutrition" on it in basic black letters. Under that in green letters it said, "Genesis 1" because that is where God says He made all the plants and seed-bearing fruits for humans to eat. This excited me and made me want to find more verses to put on shirts. Another exciting thing was that my name wasn't on it. These were sacred scripts that were straight from the Bible and gave good advice.

Here's a little bit on the process of how the "VIEW" fashion line came to be:

1. I needed a name for the fashion line. The Holy Spirit led me to make a logo from the word "VIEW". Each letter in the word "VIEW" is like a cutout from one of my book covers. Each cover was a different color so that made for a cool logo design and one that would easily be trademark

protected because it used the book covers in a series I wrote.

2. I found a print-on-demand company and began throwing designs on it that came to mind.

3. "Snitches get Stitches" is a design from King David. The corresponding verse written below it is the part in the Bible where history tells us David had a habit of raiding a city and killing all the men, women and children. His rationale was that he didn't want any survivors to be able to tell on him. These simple, sacred script designs became fun and a game for me. Within a month or so I had about 15 of them.

4. I was looking at online tee shirts and seeing they all had front designs that were catchy in some way; but none went that extra mile to make it unique like the ones I was designing. The other thing I noticed was they didn't take the time to make it a

private-label. That requires putting your logo on the inside neck and based on your design, that adds to the base price of the shirt. Doing that one inner-neck thing increased the price of my shirt and I was a little nervous at first.

5. God is creative and wants everything that represents Him to be creative as well. Like you and me. In the spirit of creativity, the Holy Spirit led me to put the "VIEW" logo on the left sleeve. That made my shirt designs stand out a little more.

6. I was happy finding creative ways to put helpful Bible verses on shirts and make them look good. The Holy Spirit let me know the shirts weren't creative enough yet. He actually told me through a couple of channels. I have a friend named Charlie I had met at Guiding Light. I showed him my first couple designs and he said they were too basic and boxy. I took his advice and looked for more

avenues to make the front designs stand out. I was using basic designs you can buy for 2$. The Holy Spirit quickly let me know Charlie was right and that we needed to step the design game up.

7. I went online and met a designer out of Florida. I gave him my view for the design that is now that book cover for "Monkey's Blood". That design took us a while of going back and forth until we found a system: I tell him what I want and he adds his creative view and shoots me a basic picture of it and I tell him what to change and it's a green light.

8. During one month, I told Netta that I believed God wanted me to go all out and invest in His fashion line. Without hesitation she agreed. We called my designer every other day with a new idea. He was like, "You guys are crazy...but the shit is hot!!" In one month we spent our savings on getting new designs. During that month though, we came up

with the hottest designs on the planet! Every design had a Bible message as well as the scripture where you can find the basis for the design.

9. I was content that the fashion line was boldly representing the Bible and God and were actually shirts I would buy from a store and wear. The Holy Spirit wasn't done with the line yet.

10. I began telling my wife and our designer that the name "sacred script" was in my head for some reason. I wasn't sure why until the Holy Spirit said, "You need to make a unique class for your shirts. Since they are scripture-based and all scripture is sacred, how about "Sacred Script". I went back through every shirt I had and added the words "Sacred Script" to the right sleeve. Now the shirts really stood out with the unique front designs and logs/patches on both sleeves!

11. In essence, within two months, we had a lineup of shirts that we knew would take the fashion world by storm. By June of this year, we had over 100 designs. We were led to cut it down to about 40 or so. We are very happy with it. We followed what God told me to do and go for broke investing in it...and as of this writing July 20, 2021, we haven't really had any sales. We've been buying them ourselves because we love them and want to wear them. We are calm and confident it will be one of, if not the number one, selling tee shirt in the industry.

12. I let my wife know that I asked Jesus to help make this the number one line in the world. I want this unique and highly fashionable brand to not only be fashionable, but instructional. I want people to look at the shirts and know there is a verse that represents not only the unique design, but it has a

helpful message backed by historical facts over time. People tell us all the time that we should be marketing them this way and that way and that real fashion designers do it a certain way. The beauty of our business model is we don't follow the rules in play. We follow the Holy Spirit's guidance and He will ensure that the same creativity and success God had in creating this diverse universe will be displayed in every area of our business ventures.

One of our designs is called "Serpent Killer". The image is of a sexxxy black female warrior holding the body of a huge snake. The snake is partially wrapped around her and its head is cut off. She has one foot on the ground and the other foot is on the severed head of the snake. The sacred script under that design is Genesis 3:15 that mentions how the woman will have a seed who will one day crush the serpents (Satan) head.

That is my wife's favorite verse and motto. We took a picture of her and sent it to our designer. He then had it made into the current design on our shirt. Jonetta Yff officially became a superhero in her own right as well as in a television series. When we had that design made, we were just beginning to talk about a making a possible television series based on my book "Kings, Queens and Killers" and give the series that same name. That's where the fashion chapter ends and the television series begins.

CHAPTER FIVE

"Kings, Queens and Killers" - the series

The plans for a television series has a background story similar to the books, podcast and fashion line: fed up. We had been watching television and commenting on the lack of substance the "boob-tube" was providing. We talked about how sex and fake-violence were selling points for most of the shows. I was starting to get fed up with the way shows were showing homosexual activity. The producers were doing to people involved in homosexual activity what they did to black people: they began to make sure each show had one representation of what they (the producer) wanted the portrayal of a certain group of people to be.

In the case of homosexual activity, the producers were making it the norm to have every show with a flamboyant type LGBT person in it. I have been talking with some people in that community and they don't like that stereotype in the same way black people didn't like being stereotyped as being stupid, slow or just like an ignorant waiter or busboy. I was enjoying a television series called "Chicago" until...until they started showing a homosexual couple with the usual stereotypes and showed the masculine female about to have "sex" with her lover and showed her walking around naked with her titties showing wearing a strap-on dick. That show is also rated pg-13 I believe.

The point is, the media has a lot of influence on society and especially young, impressionable minds. Since God already let us know we are going to be in control of the "7 Spheres of Influence in Society", since media is one of those sphere, we will begin to control the media. There is no reality in reality shows. You are pushed to say the most nasty, stupid ass thing you can say to the point where you even fake fight.

Another issue we had with the media and its movies is the way angels and Christian movies are made. Most Christian movies I have seen are boring as shit! They are dull and slow-paced. Most of them depict God as an old gentle-ass man and angels as old soft-ass, cookie-baking grannies. We hate that depiction! In reality, Jesus was a beast! He didn't back down from anybody for any reason. If you recall the story of Him in the temple when history records how He turned over the tables and told everybody to get out! Does that sound like a nice, peaceful man? My wife and I dug into ancient scriptures that tell about stories from Jesus' youth and He had that same bold mentality He had as a grown man. He was making bold statements and backing them up His whole life. It's time to show the real for what it is.

When you watch movies, who do you see as being powerful? You see the bad guy. The guy who says, "I don't care if God Himself came and tried to save you...I will kill you!"

Demons are made to be as scary, muscular, massive and powerful as possible; while the good guy angels are getting their asses handed to them every other scene. It's time to tell it like it is and show how God's angels defeat Satan and his band of merry men at every turn. There are historical accounts of angels destroying entire cities; yet the media wants us to believe they are punks and incapable of helping us out in our time of need.

The actual script for the proposed series was written near the beginning of July 2021. There are about 10 scenes that are outlined. As of July 20, 2021 I haven't had any takers yet and I also haven't put in in the professional format it's supposed to be in for a producer or an agent to look at.

The main character is the "Serpent Killer" female who is on the tee shirt design based on my wife. The goal is to have "VIEW" merchandise based on a television series as well. A top-selling fashion line based on a Bible-based book series dominating the fashion industry is unheard of...until now! As usual, the beauty is that we don't have to rush it or market it how everybody says we are supposed to market it. We are developing ideas that the Holy Spirit gives us in His own way with the understanding and faith that He knows what the future holds and has God's best interest at heart. Fulfilling your purpose is a wonderful thing when you follow God's laws.

Since the series project is only about a month old, this chapter will naturally be the shortest because there is very little to say on it yet. Just know the scenes we have right now include righteous violence, historically accurate scenes, characters based on real persons and scenes acting out the beauty of engaging in married sex within your marriage.

CHAPTER SIX

Real Estate Development

There is a finite or limited amount of space on this planet. Jesus main message was for us humans to create Heaven on Earth. His messages were about how to make money and do business in such a way that you will be in control of entire economies and cities. The purpose of that is so you can control how business is done. If you are in tuned with God and His laws, your city will run smoothly; but if you aren't interested in God or His laws, corruption and chaos will result.

There are two things I mentioned that will come into play in this chapter that God has placed on my heart that I mentioned earlier. The first is the investment process called "anthroveration" and the second is the "7 Spheres of Influence in Society".

In order to be in control of cities and have them managed properly, you have to first be good with money. That is a lesson history shows us over and over, in the Bible and any economic-related book on the planet, is essential. I already told you all my plans for business are designed to give God glory. If His main purpose for humans is to create a visible Heaven on Earth...the real estate market will need to be controlled by people who are in line with God's way of thinking.

I don't have major experience in buying and selling residential or commercial property. My area of expertise is in home repair and remodeling. Regardless, the Holy Spirit has shared real estate plans with me that He wants carried out that are so far above my current paygrade it's ridiculous! That's what excites me about it as well. The only way I will be able to describe my success in real estate on the level I will be involved in it will have to give God glory. As of this writing July

20, 2021 I am renting an apartment with my wife and the two boys. I don't own any real estate. I don't have a real estate license. I don't have a pickup truck to ride around and do home repair work. I don't have enough money in the bank to buy a bird house let alone develop hotels with arenas attached to them...but God!

Anthroveration. This concept came to me when I was disgusted with the way real estate investing has been going. I touched on it briefly in an earlier chapter, but will go into more detail here and share some well-known, but little talked about, facts. In my hometown of Grand Rapids, Michigan, there is a street called Wealthy Street. It was a predominantly white neighborhood until black people began to move in. As was the case all around America: when blacks moved in, whites either burned the black family's house down or left the neighborhoods taking their businesses with them. This process is called "white flight". I won't go into a lot of detail here because my "Anthroveration: Faith-based Investing" book covers that.

The point I will make is black families moved in and tried to maintain houses that white real estate companies made blacks pay almost double the price whites purchased the same house for, white banks charged blacks higher interest rates on loans and higher house notes than the whites who previously lived in those homes; all the while, the black families were being denied access to bank capital to start businesses and denied access to jobs that generated enough income to maintain the unfairly high mortgage etc.

The result was destructive. Black families were unable to maintain the homes and the neighborhoods began to crumble. No businesses. No jobs. Illegal income became the norm. As property values dropped, rich white investors began to secretly buy the properties for extremely low prices. This typical American scenario was the case of Wealthy Street in Grand Rapids, Michigan.

I hated to watch the "progress" Grand Rapids made in the Wealthy Street area: as the white investors began to slowly redevelop the housing stock, white people now felt the area safe enough to come back to and enjoy living in $350,000 houses that were previously values at $35,000 at best. White lawyers, doctors, restaurant owners and others now decided it was a wonderful place to have their office. The city now decided it was a nice area to redo streets and put up signs that say, "pedestrians have the right of way".

This is nothing new. This has been happening all over America and it's disgusting. There are other areas in Grand Rapids that are feeling the same change or are about to. Neighborhood investment organizations funded by rich, white investors who currently can't stand the local hoods, are making plans to spend millions in redeveloping the current black neighborhoods into "white friendly" ones.

Anthroveration is a faith-based investment process that has the ability to recognize past discriminatory practices and make substantial, unbiased progress in the face of such intentional deception. Anthroveration is based on three things:

1. Anthropology. When an investor with anthroveration plans at its core comes into a target area, there must be months of observing the lay of the land. Extensive studies into the cultural norms of the current residents must be made. Understanding the roots of these cultural differences must be unveiled and diagnosed prior to any new influx of investment monies.
2. Verification. Once the cultural norms are diagnosed they must be verified as being

legitimate. There is no community on this planet that organically wants to fall into economic disarray. Verifying the legitimacy of the struggles of the current residents is key in establishing true empathy on the side of the investor and builds stronger bonds between investors and residents. These bonds undeniably will naturally result in higher profits, new economic opportunities and self-sustained community initiatives.

3. Action. When you add "tion" to a word it makes it an action word. Once all these necessary steps of discovery and relationship-building have been made it's time to take action. Any actions armed with the data and research from the previous two stages of investment are sure to be monumental, socially beneficial, highly profitable and morally acceptable.

The book "Anthroveration" covers more of the actual development plans God has placed on my plate; but I will share a few here as well:

1. Building hotels with arenas
2. Converting closed schools into year-round academies with dormitories
3. Turning churches into Bible-based finance "colleges"
4. Investments in agricultural, solar, shrimp and fish farming
5. Starting a restaurant chain with an African American cuisine
6. Restructuring current government housing funds to make them more community-investor friendly
7. Tearing down entire blocks and creating central parks within neighborhoods

8. Reusing abandoned manufacturing plants to manufacture new products on my list

To sum up the real estate development plans God has given me: they are going to be nothing short of amazing. They will all be highly profitable with the intention of truly recreating Heaven on Earth.

CHAPTER 7

Love and Hate Memoirs (Jonetta Yff)

(God's peace, grace and mercy is what kept me sane.)

Memoir One: Written at 2pm while Larry is out getting high with my van...

I'm sitting here at 2:38pm waiting and wondering what is my next move? Back in this space I don't like much. A mind space that let me think every car that passes is my van with my husband in it who left 3 hours ago saying he giving a book to his son!!! It bothers my soul that I *allowed* his ditzy ass to tell me that story!!! It makes me want to break out in a righteous anger to kick him out and let him do his own thing knowing good and well it is I the woman who has the power over the serpent! I want to be catered to without the extra baggage...but what man can do that better than my husband? I guess because he so non-chalant about so much I figured he was manning his addiction triggers well. Guess it's all an illusion. It makes me want to relapse too but then my day counter will have to reset!! I'm doing well not thinking of week 1 but day 1 too.

I cry to my daddy and I'm not afraid of who knows. I'm lost and weak and angry and still in the midst of my pain I say thank you Daddy for another stripe on my back of LONG SUFFERING. I know this too shall pass and although I want to rush through the day to get to midnight symbolism of a new day I still have to think minutes in front of me first. I still need to think of dinner and bath time. I prayed for my husband and I can do no more. I cannot worry about him and I have to think with no emotions. That's my husband and I want better for him but I cannot allow myself to go in the deep. I need to hold on to God's promise and the kids. Nope. Daddy made this man, so He can make another for me. I have to stay focused on winning back souls for Christ.

Yeah it hurts but Daddy never said it wouldn't. He did say it will be worth it so I'm looking for that! I can't allow my ditzy husband to be the cause of that. I love him but I love Daddy much more.

Memoir Two: Written the day after Larry got high and didn't come home to me…

I am Jonetta Minter and I am learning myself. A LOT has taught me in so little…like 30 minutes little. Sometimes anger want to take the lead emotion and although rightful, it's not loving. I know I am a major key in life's success so I know that has to make the enemy mad. I want to break down and glory in my pain because honestly it hurts so good. But now I have learned with Jesus help to let it go if it isn't benefitting the upbringing of Father's work. And that's it! That's it with every question, every emotion, every cause, every choice is based on: does it benefit the upbringing of God's Kingdom? Now it's 4:10pm in the afternoon and I want to be early and I don't want to be late with picking up the kid.

Memoir Three: Written on a sleepless night…

What to do when you are restless and looking at article after article…some educational, some funny and some sad! Am I supposed to be doing something else? I know finishing the blue prints are most important. I want to grind to be done with everything: birthing center, library, restaurant, retreat home, bank…even if I can get a bonus house in like my own! That would be the dopest dope. I guess I'll go to sleep now. Pray first. Love you Daddy and thank you for not leaving me hanging. Thank God I can say I have someone who like and have passion for me!

Memoir Four: Written when my husband dropped me off in Grand Rapids to get my hair done. He got high and never came back to get me. His dope dealer came and got me 6 hours late...in my van!

Dear Daddy. God. Jesus. Where do I go from here?! I feel like I'm dying where I sit. Today was an awesome day! Well at least in my head! I didn't have nothing else planned except getting my hair done at the crack of dawn, like literally at 5am. I knew the boys were home today so it was going to be glorious! Plus the sun was out! Yesssss Daddy come through with the heat!! Funny how things can change.

Thank you for your son Jesus because there was another hiccup with my husband, your son, who needs a wife! Lord God I didn't know. Hold me up because the rage, anger, betrayal, frustration, jealousy and the envy...I rebuke it all. I even called my baby daddy to make sure he was still bitter. He is...bigtime! Forgive me Jesus for my sins. My unclean thoughts. Remove the whole core out of my being! I need you more now than I ever did! I need a mother now than I could ever imagine. Maybe that's why I don't have a baby girl. I need to get myself together. I know it's a lot of pressure for us, a couple, because we are black from broken beginnings, about to rebirth a whole black nation and nobody believes us but me, you and Larry.

We are going to be the wealthiest people in the world. It's going to be nothing to us. We don't lust after money. We lust after you and place your enemies as your footstool. Daddy I want to do that...can I? I know you gave me the power to fight. You gave me weapons to use. I am your warrior princess. You can't defeat, destroy or dissipate my soul. I am daughter to the Most High. Do you know what a Father would do for a daughter who He numbers the hairs on my head? That means my Daddy knows where hair follicle #50 is.

Memoir Five: Written after my husband got high and ran up one of many tabs with his drug dealer...

Today I must think what my actions can do to cause the dominoes to fall. It seems when I'm lost and entrapped within myself, so is everyone around me! Since I'm a powerful being, is it possible I caused the "Domino Effect" in my family? I was trapped in my lust going wild all to find my husband is now entrapped in himself and cannot be reached. And my son was entrapped with himself and couldn't stop vomiting. Plus my husband's gone with the van. I am home with the uncontrollable boy and my husband has a $250 drug tab.

Memoir Six: Written after my husband and I had an argument. He wanted to take a drive to cool down and I made the whole family go. He pulled off at an exit and got out to walk home. A police stopped him and he went to jail for a warrant...

Saturday I couldn't control my emotions either. We drove 20 minutes out of Muskegon. He got out the car and proceeded to walk home. I waited stubbornly for him to come back to the van not knowing he was hitchhiking on the freeway! After driving up and down no-man's land on the highway for 15 minutes in broad daylight without seeing him, I decided to head home. I spotted a police officer and my husband! He also has a child support warrant out for his arrest. He had to do a night in jail. I know we are greater than this!

Yes we have to go through the storm. He is my husband and I don't want to abandon him now. I have to learn that it is I that can be distracted. The woman must always be by the man's side in mind, body and soul. I must not never set down my intuition. I know what I know!! Two cards, please! Yet I am still a woman of God. I still have the power not in one but in both heels to crush a serpent's skull. That's why it's imperative that the woman stays on guard. I have the power to defeat the serpent...not the man! That's why the devil wants to separate the two; especially the ones of color. There's more power in the melanin skin. But God sent someone to die to give us each back our badge of honor...our original way of life...our victory trophy...our champion belt! We have dominion and power over everything under the sun and Daddy loves His children sooooo much! I know we are some show-stoppers. We have to repent and move on. I'm sad and hurt but we will keep moving. We still have the victory! We will be of good cheer! We must keep praying and fasting! No pain...no gain!!

Memoir Seven: A note from God...

Dear Netta,

Don't worry about the outside of yourself! You prayed and it's done. You can't change the past, can't predict the future, you are only in the right now! And right now Satan wants you, the woman, distracted. You need to focus on finishing all of your duties now! You cannot worry about Larry. He is my child...my problem. Keep being loving, kind and keep righteously stepping on the serpent's skull not just for you and your family; but for all of my people. Even your enemies!

Love God...

Memoir Eight: After another episode pre-marriage...

Why couldn't you make it back to me? I wanted to surprise you with us doing a podcast tonight. I won't say much cause I'll be speaking from a hurt place. But they playing you, having you work for them to then get in the hole to buy drugs. All your money is still with them and you still keekeein' in they face while Satan using them to get to you. He cracking up!!

Yeah God can heal and forgive you, but you still must face consequences. I need to not be attached so I don't get burned when you put me under your feet and take off running. Yeah, first time shame on you...second time shame on me; but the third time momma saying don't be no fool, fool. The heart mostly deceitful has done it again. I put myself out there again. Dived out head first just to find out the water is extremely shallow how sway! Head damaged. Heart feel foolish. Mind on a thousand. Tear drench shirt. Red bloodshot eyes. Wearing a fashionable noticeable sadness that only the good Lord God can heal!

We was stopping our addictions together and you went without me. Without a care in the world for me. You don't care or love me. It's all a part of your fantasy. It's an illusion. I'll just rather you have someone get your stuff or ill drop it off in Grand Rapids. I don't want to come to the Heights because God need me focused. You can be replaced. I can't pick you over Daddy never.

You need him and I need me better! This isn't good. I just got out of something toxic. Thank you Jesus for your grace and mercy. I fall to my knees seeking your face asking...no begging you to forgive me. Take my pain away so I don't kill myself and leave my kids parentless. Help me Holy Ghost to keep my eyes stayed on you. Help me to not turn my heart cold and put up a shield because so many people need, searching, wanting my unconditional love. And I know father, you have someone for me who will make me a number one priority! Who will protect me at all cost! Who will treat my children as their own. I need someone who is capable of being a dependable man. The thoughts that I think are good and I am constantly asking God to forgive me because if the Hulk come out of me I ain't going down without a fight. Sooooooo ready to set fires and watch my powers force it to burn it. I am love. I am kindness. I am peace. I am joy. Someone will see that I am royalty and that I am a Queen, someone they will cherish for the rest of their days on earth.

Memoir Nine: Yet another episode where the pain was once again on "10"...

As I make call number 79, my eyelashes drenched, eyes bloodshot red, cheeks with stained tears. As I UNCONSCIOUSLY hang up just to redial, my mind wonder back to the missed trigger my fiancé just gave me. He had just got finished with a friend's house doing handyman work, when he called and asked if HE CAN go see his son for an hour. Me not listening to hear that he is loading the gun to fire, I hesitate and say "yes".

Now I'm sitting 9 hours later punching myself, hurting all over when I realize God my father said give Him all the pain, all the worry, all the hurt and I honestly had to give it all to Him. Did I mention I was pregnant and our wedding is in 27 days! But God!!

CHAPTER 8

You Got That? (Larry Yff)

(In addiction…everything is linked to addiction.)

Turn

1. We're getting coked up at a pool hall.

2. I take my turn.

3. When I'm done, I step out the bathroom and one of them goes in to take a turn.

4. I grab a pool stick and take my turn.

Mafia Strip Club

5. I'm coked up and don't give a fuck.

6. I'm horny and want to see some strippers.

7. Fuck the mafia!

8. Why can't I touch her?

9. Come closer

10. Turn around

11. Bend over

12. Let me put this $20 in your bikini and touch your ass.

13. I'm coked up and don't give a fuck that this is a mafia-run club!

Bus

14. Alright. Give me $2,000 and I'll make that run right quick.

15. I'll be on the Greyhound, so give me a week.

16. I'm sniffing coke on the bus.

17. Nobody's on the bus but me and the hot chick.

18. I flash my cash.

19. She sits next to me.

20. It's dark. Nobody's looking.

21. We sniff a couple grams of blow.

22. She blows me.

23. I'm on the Greyhound

Short

24. I know it's short, but that's what I got.

25. The price was higher than I expected.

26. The quality is good though.

27. You straight?

28. Cool.

House Sitting

29. Yeah, I just wanna chill at your house for the weekend.

30. It's nice. It's empty. You're gonna sell it anyways.

31. We good? Cool.

32. "You got that? Here I come."

33. This is a cool ass backyard to get high in!

34. The breeze is a little strong.

35. Hope it don't blow my blow off this plate.

36. I'm almost out.

37. "You got that? Here I come."

Baby Sitting

38. Yeah. I'll chill for the weekend and watch your kid.

39. He knows me. We good.

40. "You got that? Here I come."

41. I wanna watch pornos in the bedroom.

42. He wants to watch kid movies in the living room.

43. I'm watching pornos in the bedroom.

44. Last night was a long one.

45. "You got that? Here I come."

46. I lost all my money playing poker!

47. Front me an 8-ball.

48. "You still need that? Here I come."

49. Slow down!

50. Too late!

51. Pull this mutha fucka over!!

52. I have to run back towards the house somehow!

53. "I'm just taking a walk officer".

54. In the back of the police car with another dope case.

55. Aw man! The kid!?!

<u>Third Shift</u>

56. "Yeah. I'm here by myself all night. You got that? Come through."

57. I don't feel like working anymore.

58. I'll pay you in coke to finish.

59. Open your shirt some more.

60. Stay bent over just like that!

61. "You want some more of that?"

62. Third shift.

Shootin' Craps

63. You don't have any more money?

64. I'll play you for that dope.

65. It's as good as money.

66. What am I gonna do with all this crack?

67. "You want me to try that?"

68. No more crack.

Hot Tub

69. I love hot tubs.

70. "You want me to bring that?"

71. Don't get the fuckin' plate wet!

Night Club

72. I love this club.

73. "You got that?"

74. It's hot in here.

75. Turn the air condition on.

76. "Were there a lot of fine honeys in there?"

Wood Floors

77. I'll sand and stain them for $500.

78. "You got that? Here I come."

79. I'll sand and stain the other floors for $250 just for you.

Cutting Trees

80. "You got that? Here I come."

81. I'll just cut the trees tomorrow.

82. "You still got that?"

83. My chainsaw ain't working.

Parking Lot

84. "Yeah we got that. Here we come."

85. Pull in backwards.

86. Move over there.

87. Pull straight ahead.

88. Is somebody in that car over there?

89. Park over there and just pull straight ahead.

90. We gotta leave.

91. We'll leave in a minute.

Leaky Roof

92. "I'll fix it for that. I gotchoo."

93. I'll finish the rest tomorrow.

94. "You got that? Here I come"

95. My truck ain't starting.

96. I'll be back to finish when I get it running. I gotchoo.

97. "You got that? Here I come."

Who is it?

98. "Yeah, I got two of 'em. Here I come."

99. Keep yours on safety.

100. That was crazy!

101. I told you I gotchoo.

102. "Let me get some of that."

Casino

103.   I'm on fire tonight!!

104.   "You got that? Here I come."

105.   I need some gas money. "You got that?"

Truck

106.   "You got that? Here I come."

107.   Let me get that then you can use it.

108.   "Where you at? You comin?"

109.   Let me get that then you can use it again.

It's yours.

110.   "You got that? You comin'?"

111.   If you want it you can get it.

112.   It's brand new.

113.   "You still got that? You comin'?"

You sure?

114.   "He got that? Here I come."

115.   You were right.

Last Time

116.   "You got that? Here I come."

117.   Last time.

118.   "You still got that? Can *you* come?"

119.   Last time.

120.   "You still up?"

121.   Last time.

122.   "I know. You coming?"

123.   Last time.

124.   "You have reached the voicemail of...."

Made in the USA
Monee, IL
14 October 2021